Firebird and Trans Am

Bill Holder and Phil Kunz

Firehawk

MOTORBOOKS

First published in 2002 by Motorbooks, an imprint of MBI Publishing Company, 380 Jackson Street, Suite 200, St. Paul, MN 55101-3885 USA

Motorbooks titles are also available at discounts in bulk quantity for industrial or sales-promotional use. For details write to Special Sales Manager at MBI Publishing Company, 380 Jackson Street, Suite 200, St. Paul, MN 55101-3885 USA

Library of Congress Cataloging-in-Publication Data Available

ISBN-13: 978-0-7603-1165-3
ISBN-10: 0-7603-1165-X

On the front cover: Although 20 years apart, each of these Trans Ams highlights the catchy style for which the model is known. Owned by Ron and Carol Lutterbie, a 1979 model is in the foreground, backed by the 1998 version.

On the frontispiece: The lettering on the hood scoops says it all on this 1975 Firebird, indicating the presence of 400-ci ram-air power under the hood that is capable of 345 horsepower.

On the title page: Starting in 1992, it was possible to acquire the SLP Firehawk version of the Trans Am. Firehawks, including this beautiful 2002 model, carry aftermarket performance, racing, and suspension upgrades.

On the back cover: The 1970 Firebird received a completely new look and a consensus thumbs-up from the buying public. Front-end changes included single headlights and a new-look Endura body color grille. The Formula 400 model shown here features a fiberglass hood and stylish scoops. When either of the ram-air engines were used with the 1970 Firebird, the ram-air identification was carried on the front hood scoops.

Edited by Chad Caruthers
Designed by LeAnn Kuhlmann

Printed China

Contents

Acknowledgments

We would like to thank the following individuals for providing their cars for photographing: Ron and Carol Lutterbie, George Clark, Rod Montgomery, Jerry Minor, Dean Pringle, Jeff Walker, Greg Jacobs, Al Bowman, David Pennington, Robert Blair, Lynn Hayworth, Shane Thompson, Charles Leavell, Jerry Beaumont, Steve Passwater, Joe Kidwell, Bob Jordan, Andy Allen, and Dave Logston.

Thanks as well to the following people for their contributions: Paul Zazarine, editor, *Pontiac Enthusiast Magazine*; Tony Sapienza, Lisa Gooth, and Jeff Romack, Pontiac Motor Division Public Relations; Jim Mattison, Pontiac Historical Services; Sarah Chandler, Performance Marketing; Fred Simmons, General Motors Drag Racing; Sue Emmel, Trans Am Club of America; Jody Messinger, SLP Engineering; David Tucker; and Darrell Willrath.

Foreword

The Pontiac Firebird and Trans Am have always been about image, and for the past 35 years they've represented performance combined with Pontiac's flair for sophistication. Right from the beginning, when Pontiac got the green light in 1965 to share the new F-body with Chevrolet, the Firebird was engineered with better suspension tuning, larger wheels and tires, and a more upscale interior trim than its bow-tie cousin, the Camaro.

The Magnificent Five packaging of the Firebird lineup gave each model an image of sophistication, from the European-imaged overhead-cam six to the muscular Firebird 400.

Pontiac's marketers were good at creating image and mystique—the GTO was proof of that—and they chose to apply the same strategy to the Firebird. It worked.

When the Trans Am arrived in 1969, it was originally a "hype" designated to draw attention to the Firebird lineup. It stood shoulder to shoulder with its GTO Judge cousin at Riverside for the automotive press to examine, and for the most part, the press didn't get the message. The Trans Am, with its spoiler and scoops and stripes, was a spoof on the musclecar movement, but it also had the hardware to back up its message of, "Hey, I might look silly, but I'll beat you on the street."

The choice of the name Trans Am was a good one, even if in its production form the car didn't meet SCCA homologation rules. The incredible redesign of the 1970 Trans Am totally changed the car's image: it looked like it belonged on the racecourse. Pontiac's advertising boasted the Trans Am had "scoops that scoop and spoilers that spoil," and that it was now a legitimate performance sports car. And with the lineage of 455 HO and Super Duty engines, the Trans Am's image was as solid as its quarter-mile performance.

But the performance market was dying in the early 1970s, and when a United Auto Workers strike halted production and left 1972 models on the line unfinished even as the time drew near for the 1973 models, the Firebird and its Camaro cousin were facing the corporate ax. Sales were soft and it seemed wiser to eliminate the car. But thanks to impassioned pleas from Alex Mair at Chevrolet and Bill Harrison and Bill Collins at Pontiac, General Motors management chose to keep the cars in production.

That decision turned out to be one of the best that GM management made in the 1970s. Sales slowly rose as the decade progressed. Even as performance cars disappeared, thanks to the movie *Smokey and the Bandit*, the Trans Am left an indelible stamp on American culture. By the late 1970s there were only two performance cars available—the Trans Am and the Corvette. One automotive magazine observed that "the Trans Am's screaming chicken is now the most recognized car emblem in the world." The Trans Am's halo effect sold hundreds of thousands of bread-and-butter Firebirds.

The automotive marketplace has changed considerably since the 1970s, and the Trans Am became a victim of GM's inability to meet the market dynamics. While the 2001 WS6 Ram Air Trans Am is far superior to the Mustang GT, it continues to lag far behind in sales. There's no question that the market for rear-wheel-drive V-8 performance cars is large enough to support the F-car.

The 35th anniversary edition that closes out the Firebird's model run is Pontiac's final statement on its long-running musclecar. The 10th, 20th, 25th, and 30th anniversary models were milestones, and to commemorate the end of the Firebird's lineage, the Trans Am has been designated to carry the 35th anniversary package.

—*Paul Zazarine, editor,* Pontiac Enthusiast *magazine*

Chapter One

The Firebird
and Trans Am

Through the years, the Firebird and its Trans Am brother have been extremely popular sports cars that have attracted a wide variety of buyers, admirers, and enthusiasts. From baby-boomers to their children, people have been drawn to the Firebird's and the Firebird Trans Am's exhilarating power and pleasing design, which have helped both carve out a unique spot in American automobile history.

As the sun rises on the new millennium, though, it appears to be setting on this distinct era of automobile. The musclecar concept has fallen out of favor, pulling aside for the more popular ideas of front-wheel-drive and sport utility vehicles. At present, it appears that the

The evolution of the Firebird's front-end design is clearly shown when these then-and-now models are parked

2002 Firebird and Trans Am models will be the final version of this Pontiac muscle legend.

What a pity for all, particularly for the Firebird and Trans Am enthusiasts, most of who would agree that the looks and performance of the current models are now about as stunning as can be achieved with a factory-built model. But wouldn't you know: The buying public's interest has turned a different direction. Such is "progress." Nevertheless, the roaring and colorful existence of the Firebird and Trans Am will live on strong.

Evolution

The competition that faced the Firebird upon its introduction in 1967 was awesome. There was the ultra-successful Ford Mustang, which had a two model-year lead, as well as competition from the similarly styled Camaro. Both were formidable competition by anyone's standards.

Motivations for the development of the Firebird were many, with the primary reason being the super-success of the Mustang, which proved beyond a shadow of a doubt that the concept of a musclecar was a viable one.

The GTO design influence is clearly evident when you put the two 1968 front ends side by side. Note the similarities of the hood scoops and the distinctive front-end shaping of the two models.

10

This 1972 Firebird shows its macho front-end design, which was extremely popular during its heyday. Without doubt, that look still remains popular today. Those classy hood scoops have returned to the modern Firebird/Trans Am design, with the 2001 model carrying a pair of very similar scoops.

For certain, Pontiac's brass didn't like their faces being rubbed in the dirt by that Ford Motor Company pony, so it was time for action. Pontiac big guns John DeLorean and Bunkie Knudson turned their attention to building a Mustang competitor—and things moved quickly. The Firebird was developed and built out of a need to prove that Pontiac could compete in this new arena.

The legendary DeLorean made it very clear that he wanted a two-seater, which could, in addition to standing alone, provide an economic alternative to the Corvette. Though GM didn't want the Firebird to compete against the company's star performer, DeLorean's point was taken. The XP-833 concept design was born.

The XP-833 was a sleek beauty, its design far ahead of its time—maybe a bit too far. The concept design looked more like it should have been competing at the Indianapolis 500 as opposed to cruising the streets. It featured a torpedo-style body and, had it been produced, may have provided more of a surprise in the industry than the 1953 Corvette did. Had the XP-833 actually become the Firebird, it could well have set a new direction for the sports car business.

Things abruptly went another direction, however, when General Motors decided that, for economic reasons, the Firebird would have to share sheet metal with the Camaro. Individual model styling be damned—the almighty dollar would be saved with this arrangement. Pontiac took this decision as a slap in its design's face, but the decision was final. Everyone knew right then that as the two designs evolved, there would be great similarities between the Firebird and Camaro. That certainly proved to be the case for many years to come.

The initial Camaro body lines were for the most part already defined, so there wasn't much room for input from the Pontiac boys. It was a squeeze-fit situation for Pontiac to incorporate its unique look with only the nose and tail areas to work with. Even the Camaro fenders had to be used.

It was clear that one thing was critical to succeed, however: The Firebird could not simply look like a reformed Camaro. Looking back, Pontiac engineers unquestionably did one heck of a job giving that first Firebird its own look. Even though there were great similarities between the two models that first year, each seemed to have its own distinctive style.

Even as performance was dropping like a rock in the early 1970s, Pontiac came forth with a full-race mill—the 455 Super Duty power plant—that was capable of almost unbelievable performance. This engine was available during the 1973 and 1974 model years.

Viewing the initial Firebird front end, it is easy to discern that there was a lot of GTO influence in place—a whole lot! It actually appeared to many that the GTO front end had been scaled down to fit the Firebird. But there was a classic look to it, with chrome circling the twin headlights and that distinctive split-grille design. The rear end also had a unique look. When you got right down to it, the Firebird was a little more highbrow than its Chevy sibling.

Eras of Distinction

While some break down the Firebird's reign into four eras, others break it into five: 1967–1969, 1970–1976, 1977–1981, 1982–1992, and 1993–2002. There is really nothing sacred about these time periods, and for the most part each era is based on similarities in design

and appearance and not necessarily by like power trains.

The original era of the Firebird was essentially a combination of elements from the Camaro and GTO, plus some subtle yet distinct characteristics of its own. The 1970–1976 time period saw the models' shapes cleaned up, with the introduction of the Endura rubber grille, single headlights, and a tapered tail. There was certainly a race car look about these models.

The 1977–1981 period saw a more conservative look for the Firebird and Trans Am, a look that went along with the reduced horsepower of the period.

With the introduction of the 1982 model, there was no doubt that this was the start of something big. A sleek new front end really set it apart from previous Firebirds. The design period also applied space-age engineering and a less-beefy design. The final period of development commenced in 1992 and continues today—for now. The styling took a giant step upward with curved styling and reinvigoration of the under-the-hood performance.

Design

The designs of the Firebird and Trans Am have progressed through the years, as the model has seen many faces and looks. The Firebird family embraced different characteristics to keep up with the times, adopting variations to create a sports car aura, aggressive musclecar looks, big-block high performance under the hood, aerodynamic styling, and often, the look of a machine that belonged on the racetrack.

The 1990s saw some sleek automotive designs, and the Firebird and Trans Am were out in front, in many minds. This factory photo shows a bright yellow 1993 Trans Am doing its thing on a winding road. In addition to their sharp appearance, these modern models also had great performance and handling. *Pontiac*

Firebird and Trans Am have always had a racing image, and it has best been manifested in a number of both Indianapolis 500 and NASCAR pace cars. The 1989 Indy 500 pacer, in the form of the Twentieth Anniversary Trans Am, was a detailed-out Trans Am with the race identification on the doors. *Pontiac*

Even with those difficult initial design constraints and tough competition, the Firebird line has survived the years and weathered numerous tough times along the way. No longer a Camaro hanger-on, the Firebird and its flashy Trans Am offshoot continued to take on their own personality and move in a different direction to carve their own spot in American automobile history.

Of course, the Trans Am has always been the top model in the Firebird line. Through the years, though, the Trans Am has evolved to become a completely separate model. Most owners of this classic line will tell you that they have either a Firebird or a Trans Am. Enough said!

Performance

Appearance has without question been a strong suit of the Firebird line, but performance was also immediately evident in the initial Firebird model. The power plant was a 326ci mill, which sported a four-barrel carburetor, dual exhausts, and a 10.5:1 compression ratio that put down an impressive 285 horses.

But that was just the beginning. More horsepower would follow, coming from big-block engines, including the original 400, which put out 325 horses. With a relatively light car at a ton and a half, you can believe that these models could really got it on! Things kept perking, though. The horsepower roared to 345 with the ram-air power plants.

During the exciting performance era of the late 1960s and early 1970s, the Firebird model never seemed to assume a true musclecar image. It's hard to understand why, because many versions of both the Firebird and Trans Am certainly qualified. But most of the models that carried the muscle image were medium-size sedans, while the Firebird models had more of a sports car image.

Of course, no conversation about the Firebird and Trans Am's performance would be complete without mentioning the unforgettable Super

Duty models of 1973 and 1974—a time when, as a whole, the performance era declined. The Super Duty engine was rated at a conservative 290 horsepower, which was obviously a joke. This was a pure race mill that was built like a competition engine. These SD models are considered to be some of the top Firebird collectibles. In addition, a number of the ram-air models of the late l960s—specifically of the 1969 and 1970 vintage—have serious collector appeal.

But with the exception of the Super Duty model years, the Firebird line experienced a plummet of power under the hood, like most other cars, during the gas-crunch days of the 1970s and even into the 1980s. The performance, however, did come back big time in the 1990s, with the LS1 and later the LT-1 small-block power plants, which would see horsepower soar past the 300 mark, with the 2002 model reaching an awe-inspiring 325!

Racing 'Til the End

High performance is one reason that the Firebird line has always had a race connotation. With names like Formula (as in Formula 1) and Trans-Am (as in the SCCA Trans Am racing series), and with a race version of the Firebird actually competing in that latter race series, it's no wonder. During the 1960s and running all the way into the 1980s, the sleek Firebird design was many times selected as an oval track race performer.

In addition, the Firebird body style serves as the basis for the race car used in the International Race of Champions (IROC) series. It has also been the Indy 500 Pace Car on a number of occasions, and has served as a NASCAR pacer at many tracks during the 1990s.

The styling and performance of the Firebird and Trans Am have been at the forefront of the American automotive industry for 35 years, with a number of the designs and power plants receiving raves—and high sales—from the buying public. The Firebird, with its top Formula model, and

In the mid-1990s, Pontiac made huge advertising use of the Firebird's selection as the vehicle to be used in the International Race of Champions (IROC) series. The cars were built as identically as possible, and the greatest drivers in the world raced them in four national races. *Pontiac*

the Trans Am, with high-tech models like the GTA, have had a number of special models through the years that are classics today.

The Firebird and Trans Am. Two enduring icons that represent the American road and racetrack in all its glory. Each has a history worth remembering, and they are chronicled in the pages to follow.

Chapter Two

1967-1969

The first three Firebirds and the initial Trans Am came on like gangbusters and really caught the fancy of the buying public. That was just the beginning of things to come.

1967

This year's car was the inaugural model. And as such, the 1967 l/2 Firebird is considered to be one of the most valuable of the Firebird fleet. For a first-year automobile, there was an amazing selection of models, power plants, and options. Buyers could choose from a flood of interior options, three different types of wheel discs and a pair of Rally wheels, many types of power assists, and air conditioning. It was a trend that would continue with Firebirds through succeeding years.

Even though Pontiac was forced to adhere to already-existing Camaro sheet metal, the inaugural Firebird managed its own distinct look. The characteristic split front-end design, along with the black-out hood, gave it a unique look.

Obviously, the public liked what it saw, and it bought more than 82,000 units of that first Firebird. It was a significant sales accomplishment considering that the model had a monstrously late February introduction!

Pontiac used the Firebird's great option selection with an advertising blitz that asked potential buyers, "Which Firebird Is for You?" Pontiac also tried its best to divorce the model from its obvious Camaro heritage. It marketed the Firebird as a distinctive, on-its-own sports car, hitting particularly on the styling and performance aspects of the new model.

When you viewed the model from the side, that Camaro look was undeniably present. But in the front and rear treatments, Pontiac engineers established an elegant appearance, including the Pontiac GTO-style front with horizontally mounted lights resting within the recesses of the distinctive black-out grille. When you remember that all this design had to be accomplished within tight design constraints, the result was truly amazing. It wasn't how Pontiac had wanted to do it, but there's no arguing that the results were outstanding.

Aft body treatment was also distinctive with four (two on each corner) horizontal taillights. The Pontiac identification was carried in the lower center of the rear deck. There was also the HO body style, which carried the model identification in a body-length stripe. The Sprint model that was in place the first model year also gained a lot of appreciative attention with an economical overhead-cam six-cylinder that had surprising performance. *Road & Track* magazine tested the bottom-end model at an impressive 15.4 second quarter-mile clocking.

The first Firebird also featured big performance. The initial big-power engine was a 326ci mill (in the sporty HO version), which sported a four-barrel carburetor, dual exhausts, and a 10.5:1 compression ratio. It could put out 285 horsepower, which was merely a starting point for the big blocks to come.

The optional 326 engine made the model a real rocket, and it became one of the most desirable of the early Firebirds. It cost an extra $280 to acquire those increased ponies, but it was worth the money. Performance with the 326 mill was

Although the Firebird is usually known as a performance machine, the baseline 3.8-liter straight-six engine certainly didn't start off that way. Horsepower was only 115 with a two-barrel carburetor. More punch came with a four-barrel, but if you really wanted performance, the 326 and 400ci V-8s were the way to go.

The letters "HO" embedded in the side trim stripes identified the punchy 326HO model for the first Firebird. This model carried the high-output version of the 326ci power plant that was capable of 285 horsepower. Also included in the $181 HO package was a heavy-duty suspension and a column-mounted shifter.

such that it seemed as if the engine had been dropped off at the neighborhood speed shop, where it was fitted with a hot cam, split-exhaust manifold, low-restriction air cleaner, and a Rochester four-barrel carburetor.

For the top-dog performer of the first year 'Birds, the Firebird 400 was the hot ticket. There were actually two versions of this engine, even though both were rated at a punchy 325 horse-power. The ram-air version, which tacked on an additional $263 to the option sheet, featured functional hood scoops (nonfunctional on the standard 400 engine) and enabled the advertised horsepower to be accomplished at lower revolutions than with the base 400 version.

The top 400 power plant was very similar to the vaunted GTO power plant, but it carried a lower-lift and shorter-duration cam. The torque of both Firebird 400 engines was a stump-pulling 4l0 lbs-ft.

1968

The 1968 Firebird model looked very much like the original, as Pontiac left things pretty much status quo. Why mess with a model that the public obviously liked? You have to remember that for a new model during the 1960s time period this was a strange situation, because models seemed to change annually. It proved to be the correct call, as more than 117,000 Firebirds rolled out of the showrooms during year two.

Refinements for Firebird number two were minor in nature, with the most notable being the omission of the venerable vent windows. Along with the improved cooling that this achieved, it created an overall sleeker look for the body. Also, the Firebird lettering with the 'Bird symbol spread its wings just forward of the name tag. The interior featured wood-grain detailing on the dash and console. These were all minor adjustments to Pontiac's successful original.

Also for 1968, the Firebird 350 engine package was a new power plant carrying only a two-barrel carburetor, but it still produced an impressive 265 horsepower at 4,600 rpm. The HO displacement numbers of 1967 moved up to 350 for Firebird year two, and the performance now equaled 320 horses. The shifter was still on the column, and the performance goodies included dual exhausts, a heavy-duty battery, and F70 x 14 rubber.

These were great numbers for a small-block and close to the standard for the day of achieving a horsepower for each cubic inch. The big factors for the performance boost were the l0.5:1 compression ratio and a Rochester four-barrel.

Today's musclecar fanatics, though, will tell you that the 400ci versions (there were three in 1968) were the hot tickets. With the exception of the few 427 COPO Camaros that were produced that model year, Pontiac had a slight step up on the Camaros, with that machine's biggest mill coming in at 396 cubic inches.

The shifter for the 400 engine moved to the floor and controlled a manual three-speed for the 400ci versions. The standard package was called the Firebird 400, but to really light your fire there was the ram-air version. There was only a five-horsepower difference between the 400 engines, with the ram-air version rated at 335 horses at 5,000 rpm.

The standard 400 power plant perked at a 10.75:1 compression and carried a unique power-flex fan and a Rochester four-barrel carburetor. The FB400 wasn't cheap, though, as it required an extra $435 on the counter.

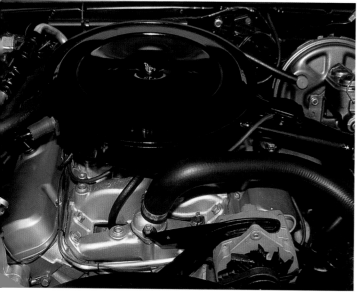

Above: There were few changes to the front end of the second Firebird. Parking lights were removed from the lower grille slots and wrapped around the front body corners. Also new in 1968 were side-marker lights on the rear flanks.

The HO designation was added to a 350ci engine package for the 1968 Firebird. The performance was impressive, with 320 horsepower coming online. Additional performance goodies included dual exhausts and a heavy-duty battery.

Thirty years difference in age exists between these 1998 and 1969 Trans Ams. The differences are stunning, but note the twin ram-air tunnels that both models demonstrate. It comes down to a matter of choice as to which model you like best.

The top dog in the 1968 performance parade, though, was the ram-air 400 version that carried oh-so-desirable twin functional hood scoops. These were supposedly all-weather devices that remained open all the time. Most owners, however, kept them closed during the winter.

A second version of the ram-air power plant was introduced near the end of the model year as the Ram Air II. It might have been called an upgrade, but it was effectively a new power plant. We're talking full-race here with four-bolt main bearings, a special manifold, and forged pistons.

21

The Firebird 350 model featured an L30 engine under the hood, bearing a 9.2:1 compression ratio and a two-barrel carburetor. Surprisingly, even during this era of high-performance, it was the most popular seller.

1969

You would have to call the Firebird's third year one of transition. You name it, and it took place in this model.

A major handling problem faced the earlier Firebird designs, and this was addressed in the 1969 Firebird. It was called wheel hop, and the problem received significant bad press with the 1967 and 1968 models. To address the situation, designers installed multi-leaf springs and staggered shocks in all models but the base one.

There was also a complete sheet metal restyling. With this restyling, the Firebird line moved away from its Camaro constraints and established itself as a distinct entity and not just a copycat of the Camaro. But even with all this going for the model, its production experienced a downturn to less than 88,000, considerably lower than the dynamite l968 sales bonanza.

To many, the 1969 front-end treatment seemed to lose some of its original style. With the headlights encased in body-color pods, the grille looked as if it had been squeezed to the center, as though it were puckering its lips for a kiss!

The front fenders were equipped with stylish wind splits and the body was given a slightly lower profile. The wheel openings were flattened at the top, which was a noticeable design deviation from the rounder styles of the earlier model years. A choice of hoods was also available this model year, with the integral scoop version available with the powerful ram-air power plants.

New interior designs were also a highlight of this last-of-the-decade model. The dash design was all new, which made for better monitoring by the driver. Even a very unsporty bench seat, though a rarity in the Firebird, was available. But

New grille treatment marked the 1969 Trans Am front end. Twin headlights were no longer surrounded by chrome; now only the twin-opening grille was so encased. Lexan plastic was used for the first time in this front-end treatment. The model was available only in the blue and white color scheme shown here.

The more powerful Ram Air IV (345 brake horsepower) was an option with the 1969 model and added only $77 to the purchase price.

Moving up another performance step, there was the Ram Air 400 L74 (option 348) power plant. The engine was basically a refinement of the aforementioned W-66 mill. The L74 power plant used the hood scoops for their intended purposes and also included a special declutching fan. But the induction only raised the horsepower five horses over the baseline 400, to 335 ponies. The torque of the two engines was actually the same, at 340 lbs-ft. There has always been confusion with this power plant, since it was also called the Ram Air III and the 400HO, but it was all the same engine system. It was actually only the number two power plant for this one model year, however.

The ultimate deal, though, for this model year was the last and best—the Ram Air IV. The L67 power plant in this package was similar to the W-66 and L74 mills, but it incorporated valve train changes and a hotter cam. The result was an additional 10 horsepower—to 345 at 5,400 rpm—though an identical torque figure.

Every owner wanted it known when he had a Ram Air IV under the hood, a fact that was denoted by lettering on the functional hood scoops. These ram-air power plants, as was true

who'd want a bench seat with a muscle sports car of this caliber?

In the performance department for 1969, the HO nomenclature was added to the 350 numerals, and tons of ready power came onboard. The L76 350ci engine (option 434) pounded out a big blocklike 325 ponies at 5,100 rpm. A reworked cam and valves were the important internal parts, turning the machine into a solid 15-second performer in the quarter.

The base big-block model was the Firebird 400 (option 345 W-66). At 330 horses, it provided only five more ponies than the 350HO but provided much more torque—430 lbs-ft, versus 380 for the 350HO.

throughout the years, could be acquired with a majority of the Firebird and Formula models—and with the top-of-the-line Trans Am, which was the other half of the story of 1969.

The Trans Am

It wasn't a great start for the new model, with the Sports Car Club of America (SCCA) racing group threatening legal action over the use of the name of its racing series. It would later be resolved with Pontiac paying the group five dollars for every Trans Am sold.

The Trans Am sheet metal was the same as the Firebird line, but the detailing and appearance styling really set it off. In fact, through the years, the Trans Am would adopt a personality and identity of its own. Officially, it was the Firebird Trans Am, but for practically everybody that owned one, it was simply the Trans Am.

But even with the lawsuit and the late model-year introduction, there were early indications that the Trans Am was going to be something big, even though the original production totals that first year were not encouraging.

Driving down the road, you could not mistake that first Trans Am when it came at you. Each had the same paint scheme: Cameo White with twin blue stripes that swept the length of the car. Other highlights in the styling included a dual-scoop hood, which, besides having a great look, was also functional; air extractors on the

The Ram Air III (or 400HO) power plant, shown here, was the number-two power plant for the Firebird and Trans Am for the 1969 model year. The gutsy mill was a favorite with the performance-buying public and had a factory rating of 335 horsepower.

front fenders; and a rear-deck spoiler that showed a GTO heritage. All together, the package was definitely a preview of things to come.

The high-performance power plants were available, with the Ram Air III being the standard mill. The ultimate machine, though, was a Ram Air IV under the hood of your Trans Am. Should you have been lucky enough to own that desirable combination, it would be proudly announced for you with lettering on the functional hood scoops. Production numbers of the Ram Air IV were very low, however. In the case of the Trans Am, only 55 were produced. One can but imagine the ever-increasing value of those particular Trans Ams that still remain.

Chapter Three

1970-1976

The new looks of the 1970 Firebird and Trans Am signaled a new goal for sales of both models. Pontiac was aiming to compete with higher-level competition than the Mustang. The lines were slick and clean. The rear spoiler was no longer a hang-on appendage, but molded into the rear deck.

This era had moments, however, when the very existence of the line was in question. In response to the federal government's crackdown on high-performance vehicles, plus the escalating costs for motorists to insure them, General Motors considered dropping the Firebird line in 1972. Fortunately, however, the Firebird survived, and the result was a great era.

An integral spoiler was the design highlight for the 1970 Trans Am. The smooth flaring gave the front the look of a race car. Other upgrades included improved suspension and steering, along with standard front disc brakes.

1970

The year 1970 saw a completely new realm of the Firebird come online. Actually, for the second time in four years, there was another 1/2 situation—a 1970 1/2 model—because of the late arrival of this completely restyled version. The company, though, didn't like the 1/2 nomenclature, and instead called the 1970 'Birds the 1970+ version.

The 1970+ Firebird looked smaller than its earlier brothers even though it was actually over an inch longer and a half-inch narrower than the 1969 model. The wheelbase was identical, but both the front and rear wheels were moved forward three and one-half inches.

The new-decade look was broadcast very clearly with the new names of the two top Firebirds—the Esprit and the Formula 400. Pontiac executives felt that the Firebird was now ready to compete in the worldwide market.

Designers did their job well, producing a Euro-appearing design, incorporating a perfectly integrated Endura grille combined with a sleek fastback body design. Single headlights also made their first appearance in the design.

But even with all the new looks, sales for the model were disappointing, coming in at only about half of the 1969 total, with only 45,543 models sold.

That disappointment certainly couldn't be shared with the new Firebird Formula sports model that was introduced—and sold over 7,700. The Formula had the looks and equipment to go

The 1970 Firebird received a completely new look and a consensus thumbs-up from the buying public. Front-end changes included single headlights and a new-look Endura body color grill. The Formula 400 model shown here featured a fiberglass hood and stylish scoops. When either of the ram-air engines were used with the 1970 Firebird, the ram-air identification was carried on the front hood scoops.

The Ram Air III 400ci power plant was the less powerful of two ram-air power plants for 1970. This mill sported 335 horses, only 10 fewer than the Ram Air IV version. This engine had 430 lbs-ft of torque at 3,400 rpm, the result of a four-barrel carburetor and 10.5:1 compression ratio.

with its trendy name, featuring both front and rear stabilizer bars, front disc brakes, and high-rate springs. Externally, the Formula looked like a sleek road racer with sport-type wheels and rakish styling. The long snorkel scoops swept the length of the fiberglass hood, terminating just short of the grille piece.

With the Trans Am, it was possible to get another color combination in 1970—the same color scheme as the 1969, just flipped. And that integrated front air dam and the smooth wheel well flares were dynamite! The new Endura-material fascia and air deflectors located on the front quarters had all the car magazine reporters breathless. Pontiac advertising promoted the 1970 Trans Am with the statement, "We take the fun of driving seriously."

But the crowning glory of this design was the hood. This was the first model to display that famous bird decal on the hood.

Engine air intake, however, was changed considerably with the deletion of the macho hood

scoops that gave that version its unique look. Instead, there was a rear-pointing shaker scoop with a functional flapper door. The shaker would be around for a number of years.

For the 1970 models, all three versions of the 400-powered 1969 Firebirds were replaced by the newly named 1970 Formula 400, with two versions of the mill available. The engines were actually identical to the base 400 (330 horsepower) and Ram Air III (345 horsepower) of the previous model year.

The refined Ram Air IV, which now carried the RPO code of LS1, was also available in 1970, but it had to be special ordered. Its horsepower was now kicking the performance ceiling at 370 ponies. One of these ram-air-powered machines would be a great collectible find, as only 88 were built.

1971

Click up one model year, to 1971, when only minor cosmetic changes were made to the Firebird. The biggest addition was the louver package on the front quarter panels. The flashy Esprit model was in its second year, with the Trans Am now starting year three. There was essentially no change externally in the Trans Am, though this was the model year that the polycast honeycomb wheels became a Trans Am option, a selection that quickly become trendy as many TA buyers checked it off on the order slip. The interior got an upgrade of standard high-back bucket seats.

The year 1971 was an interesting year in terms of performance for the Firebird line. All automotive books will tell you that this year marked the beginning of the end for big-horse-power engines. The new goals on the horizon were ways to address the new smog requirements and to squeeze out better mileage.

That's what was said, at least, as this year was certainly a period of contradiction for two reasons. First, in line with the new way of thinking, all 400ci engines were dropped. But then the reverse trend came online with the introduction of the new big-block 455ci engine. That huge displacement engine was the biggest displacement engine ever installed in a performance model, with both the Firebird and Trans Am recipients of the giant mill. And happiness must have reigned supreme, as the engine's displacement surpassed rival Chevy's biggest power plant, the potent 454.

Small-block engines still powered the second model year of the new decade, with the base 350 V-8 two-barrel engine providing 250 horses at 4,600 rpm. Its compression ratio was 8.8:1, which was pretty standard for the period. A downgraded 400 was also available this model year. With a two-barrel carburetor and only an 8.2:1 compression ratio, the engine put out 180 horsepower.

Before we go on, a point must be made: Horsepower numbers were now being stated in net figures, with the horsepower measured after all the accessories were installed. This resulted in lower horsepower figures. The net figure represented a brake horsepower figure (the earlier HP method), which was 10 to 20 percent higher. During 1971, all horsepower ratings carried both numbers, but in the following years, only the net numbers would be provided.

The 400ci power plant carried by the Formula 400 was down a bit from previous versions, but still potent at 300 brake horsepower (250 net horsepower) and 400 lbs-ft of torque.

But it was the pair of thundering 455s that really got the public's attention. At only an 8.2:1

The 455 was new for 1971 and it was celebrated with the 455HO power plant. The identification of the engine was accomplished by a small "455HO" decal on the shaker hood. Performance was advertised as 335 horsepower, pretty impressive performance considering that the compression ratio had been dropped to 8.4:1.

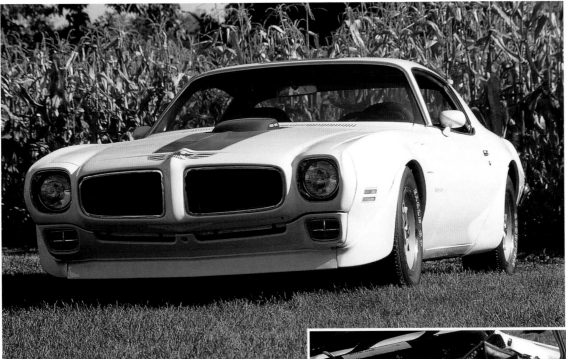

Dynamite looks continued to keep the 1972 Trans Am up front. Its body design didn't actually change that much from the previous years, but why mess with the success of such a great look? Note the prominent front spoiler.

Not only did the 1972 Trans Am's appearance set it off, but its rarity makes it a high-value collectible. The only power plant available was the impressive 455HO mill, which provided 300 horsepower and 4l5 lbs-ft of torque.

compression ratio, the less powerful 455 engine still produced 325 brake horsepower (255 net horsepower). The torque stood at an amazing 455, which exactly matched the engine displacement figures.

Then, for $237 extra, there was the killer 455HO, which was capable of 335 brake horsepower. This engine carried a four-barrel, 8.4:1 compression ratio mill , and was controlled by a floor-shifted three-speed transmission. The 455HO was also the standard engine for the Trans-Am, but find one resting in a Formula and you have found a rare machine.

1972

It did not look good for Pontiac's pony performance model in 1972. The trends in production of the model told the sad story, with sales showing a straight-line decline to less than half the 1971 figure.

The situation caused Pontiac to seriously consider completely dropping the entire Firebird line, or possibly just the Trans Am. Chevy even considered dropping its more-popular Camaro. To keep costs down after deciding to go ahead with production, there were only minimal changes made to the Firebird and Trans Am. The most noticeable difference for all versions was the introduction of the recessed honeycomb mesh grille.

The dire predictions that had preceded the 1972 model year were somewhat manifested, as only 5,249 Formulas were produced. About one-fifth of that number (1,082, to be exact) carried the manual synchromesh transmission.

The 1972 Formula was a real looker of a machine, set off by the sweeping fiberglass hood and twin air scoops traversing its length. And why change perfection? That was the rationale for keeping the Trans Am the same for year number four.

During this model year, Pontiac offered an optional Code M two-barrel 350ci V-8 power plant with a continuing-to-spiral-downward 160 horsepower, and with the net horsepower figures now becoming standard. The compression ratio continued to move away from performance, and now stood at only 8.0:1. But moving in the other direction, the Code N 350 power plant, when

Stylish air extractors and fender flairs were the highlights of the 1973 Trans Am body style. The bird decal for this model year almost completely encompassed the hood area. The graphic really helped set off the Trans Am as a unique machine.

equipped with dual exhausts, picked up 15 additional horsepower.

The L65 400ci power plant, standard with the Esprit, hooked to the M40 Turbo-Hydramatic tranny. Carrying duals, the power plant was worth an impressive 175 net horsepower. Depending on the engine choice, the Formulas were identified as the Formula 350, Formula 400, or Formula 455.

The 1972 model year also saw the continuation of the 455 engine numbers, the LS5 455-HO in particular, which was still potent, with a 300 horsepower rating and 415 lbs-ft of torque.

1973

Firebird models for 1973 sported an abundance of new internal motifs, revised colors, and slightly modified sheet metal. A new redesigned nose piece, still made of Endura, proved to be very crashworthy. The top Firebird models, including Trans Am, sported the stylish shaker hood, fender-mounted air extractors, and fender flares.

Color choices for the Trans Am increased by two this model year, with Brewster Green and Buccaneer Red coming on board.

A revolution in performance took place for 1973 with the surprising introduction of the SD (Super Duty) 455, which was ordered under RPO LS2. This was a pure-race power plant that hit the street in this most surprising time period, a time when many thought that performance was gone forever. This final performance engine of the decade could be ordered only with the Formula and Trans Am.

The SD was packed with all the good stuff, including a specially reinforced block containing forged connecting rods, aluminum pistons, dry sump oiling system, high-performance camshaft, four main bearings, and a race-style dual-exhaust system. Its factory-rated 310 horsepower was probably far underrated, with its performance more likely on the same level as the legendary ram-air engines of several

model years earlier. Interestingly, late in the model year, the SD horsepower rating was dropped 20 horses to 290. The reason for the change is not clear.

To hear the description of this engine, one would have thought that this mill was designed for the racetrack rather than for the street. Needless to say, the 252 models produced in 1973 with the SD are drawing big money from collectors in the twenty-first century.

There was also a second, downgraded-performance 455 available, the code Y L75 version, which carried a 250-horsepower rating. The reduction was mainly due to the compression ratio being lowered to 8:1. It was wildly popular, with 4,550 being sold and more than twice as many hooked to automatic transmissions.

The code M and N 350 engines (160 and 175 horses, respectively) could be ordered along with the code R L-78 400ci four-barrel power plant. The latter was rated at 250 net horsepower and could certainly stand on its own in stop-light confrontations.

1974

Design changes for the 1974 line just didn't cut it, according to Firebird/Trans Am enthusiasts. The rakish look was gone, replaced with what the wind tunnel dictated to be the design of least air resistance.

The longtime flat-nose design departed, replaced with a slant design. Twin-grille styling was still in place, but much of the pizzazz was gone.

Significant changes were made to the rear of the body. The chrome rear bumper was no more, replaced by a rubber impact strip traversing the rear and rolling around to the rear quarters on both sides. Taillight treatment consisted of the lighting stretching further inward toward the center. It was definitely a different look. The Brewster Green option was replaced by an Admiralty Blue shade.

The release of the SD-455 power plant during the era of increasing insurance and gas shortages seemed to be a contradiction. Who would have guessed that such a mill would hit the street? But for those who appreciated its performance, it was an answer to their prayers!

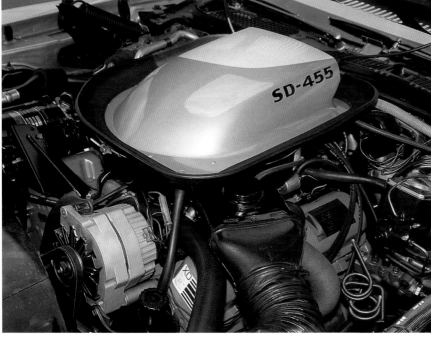

A powerhouse in a period of bland no-punch engines: That's what you would have to call the 1973 SD-455 engine. The engine could be defined as full-race, with tons of high-performance innards. Its advertised horsepower of 290 was a joke, as its 13-second performance in the quarter attested. The SD-455 power plant was available for the last time in 1974 and produced 290 net horsepower and 395 lbs-ft of torque.

The year 1974 was the Super Duty's second—and final—year. A total of 900 Trans Ams carried the brutish power plant.

The SD was still the blaster it had been the year before, with the appropriate SD-455 nomenclature on the hood-protruding shaker. As it had near the end of the 1973 model year, it carried a 290 horsepower rating. But with its high-performance innards, it continued to be a performer of monumental proportions. The quick-revving, 8.4:1 compression ratio engine brought a heart-pounding response when the pedal was slammed to the floor. The SD-455-powered Trans Ams seemed to get all the publicity, but the 43 Formulas that also carried this engine deserve their place in the spotlight as well as a candidate for the most desirable of the Firebird breed. To many, any Firebird with the SD-455 identification is the most prized Firebird performance collectible.

A lesser 455 power plant was again available with the Formula that year, with the L75 model generating 40 fewer horses than its SD brother. No slouch, the L75 could still pump out 395 lbs-ft of torque, only 15 fewer than the big boy SD-455.

A sad end to the 455 story—for both the SD and L75—came at the close of the model year, when both were dropped. It came down to the simple fact that power and performance just weren't in vogue anymore.

There were two other engines available with the Formula that year: the upgraded versions of the 350 and 400ci engines. A 170-horse version of the 350 engine, along with a 400-cube engine capable of 190 horses, provided a Formula purchaser with a considerable choice

Although the performance for the 1975 Trans Am had fallen off the table, that sure couldn't be said for the model's appearance. The Trans Am had the look of a race car, with its flashy wheel opening moldings and black-out grille.

for his performance whims. Even so, the loss of the SD after this model year was painful!

1975

The number of 1975 Firebird models was halved from the previous year to include only four—the base model, one Esprit and two Formulas, plus, of course, the Trans Am. New for 1975 was the Radial Tuned Suspension (RTS), which became standard on all models.

Not only did the 1975 Formula not have the performance capabilities of the earlier models—and in fact was not even close—the general opinion was that the looks had also deteriorated. The twin scoops seemed to look out of place with the front-end treatment of this model. Without the rear-deck spoiler, the model looked like it had been chopped off, both front and rear.

The Trans Am was detailed almost identically to the previous model year, with the exception of wraparound rear glass and movement of the parking lights to the horizontally formatted grille.

Not a single Firebird V-8 engine for the 1975 model year had an 8.0:1 compression ratio. In fact, with all the engines barely running at 7.6:1, they weren't even approaching the levels of their predecessors. The lone 455 power plant, which had been brought back by popular demand, could now only be ordered in the Trans Am, and no longer for the Formula. Rated at an anemic 200 horsepower, it was 90 horses short of the SD. The Formula line again carried the Formula 350 and Formula 400 engines. The 350

power plant carried a 175-horsepower rating and utilized a four-barrel carburetor. The L78 400 engine, rated at 185 horses, was the best you could get that year with the Formula.

This continuing downturn in power certainly had the performance-minded shaking their heads, though it was an industrywide trend. There was also really a double-whammy to what performance there was, because the lower rear-end ratios, while emphasizing economy, actually made the figures lower than they seemed.

The Super Duty power plant was gone for 1975, but externally, there were very few changes made to the body design. A new 455HO engine certainly didn't have the punch of the earlier engine of the same name. Its rating was only 200 net horsepower. The displacement numbers were still the impressive 455ci, but the power was a far cry from the good old SD days.

The 455 was on its final legs. It was soon replaced with a 400ci version. This lower-displacement engine was very popular, with several special editions in 1976. The performance was down, but for the time, it was about as good as you could get.

1976

The year 1976 was something of a landmark for the Firebird line. Changes that came to pass that year would influence the model's design direction for years to come. Most important to Pontiac, 1976 would be the first year that the production would exceed six figures, reaching 110,775.

Highly acclaimed styling changes gave the model quite a different look. The lower spoiler inlets were decreased in size, swallowing the parking lights, which had been located in the grille openings. The bumper treatment deserved a second look, as they carried body colors and provided a sweeping look to the front end.

Extensive changes, especially in the grille, retained the long-standing twin scoops, but the indentations weren't as deep as in the past. Rectangular headlights peeked out for the first time. Also, a Trans Am design change showed a broader bulge in a new hood design.

Special packages were available for both the Formula and Trans Am. The W50 option with the Formula featured a lower body stripe, blackout hood scoops, and the large Formula lettering. For the Trans Am, the Y81 Special Edition Package was appearance-oriented, while the Y82 option provided a T-top configuration. This model of Trans Am showed strong from a design aspect, with body-integrated fascias and side-splitter tailpipes.

In 1976, a huge transition took place under the hood, the first milestone being the fact that it was the final year for the 455 big block. It didn't seem to make any difference, though, as the big block was but a mere whisper of its former self. It was already gone in the Formula, but its final breath came as a performance option with the Trans Am. The once-powerful mill now sported only 200 net horsepower.

Chapter Four

1977-1981

This era introduced itself in 1977 with a front-end refinement and the return to dual headlights. The first two years also saw changes to the twin-opening grille, and another facelift occurred in 1979 with a completely new front-end look: The four headlights were recessed and separated, and the grilles were located low in the front end. It certainly gave the Firebird line a new look and moved away from what the buying public had become used to up to that point.

1977

The year 1977 was the third-best year for sales in Firebird history, with a total of l55,736 sold, surpassed only by the two previous years' totals. Another new grille design for all models retained the pair of

The 1977 Trans Am presented a new look, highlighted by its classy grille design. The two grille openings were retained, but the inner portions of the openings were curved, which provided a completely different appearance. There were also twin rectangular headlights for the first time.

openings, but the inner edges were curved for the first time. For the first time the grille openings contained the Trans Am's new quad headlights. The new cast-aluminum snowflake-design wheels really set off the front-end look.

The model year also saw the base 400 engine produce 180 horsepower, but the so-called W72 version of this engine generated an additional 20 horsepower. It took a real Firebird expert to determine which engine was under the hood, but the identity clue was that the W72 engine displayed "T/A 6.6" on the hook shaker, while "6.6 Liter" indicated that either a 400 or the new 403 engine was under the hood.

1978

Things remained relatively status-quo in 1978, with much of the 1977 design carried over. A new black-out grille in the Formula really set the model apart.

Two big-block power plants were available with the model in 1977, with both a 403ci and the W72 version of the 400ci engine. The net horsepower of the two engines was 185 and 200, respectively. The engines were denoted with "6.6 Liter" lettering on the shaker cowl.

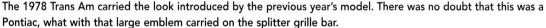

The 1978 Trans Am carried the look introduced by the previous year's model. There was no doubt that this was a Pontiac, what with that large emblem carried on the splitter grille bar.

The name of the game this model year was special editions with all the models. The Esprit came with the interestingly named Sky Bird and Red Bird Editions. Special 'Bird decal identification, custom paint, and custom interiors were featured. The Y82 and Y84 Trans Am Editions featured knockout gold and black color schemes. The Y88 Gold Special Edition has continued to hold an interest through the years and is a popular collectible.

A new 305ci Chevy-designed small-block was available for the first time in 1978. It was rated at a paltry 145 horsepower. Also available were 400 and 403ci engines, both of which generated similarly reduced capabilities.

The company made a variety of power plants available, with both a two- and four-barrel version of—for the first time—a V-6, the L37. But it was the 400 and 403 V-8 pair that still held the most attention and earned the biggest sales.

1979

The 1979 Trans Am carried a new cross-lace grille design, a black-out taillight motif, and a new lettering style on the external graphics package.

The biggest surprise with the 1979 design was the introduction of a completely new grille design for each model. Now the models looked more conventional, with a closed design bearing recessed headlights replacing the twin-opening style.

The long-standing grille tradition was finally discontinued. Many were disappointed in the movement away from tradition, but the objection was refuted with the greatest sales bonanza to date.

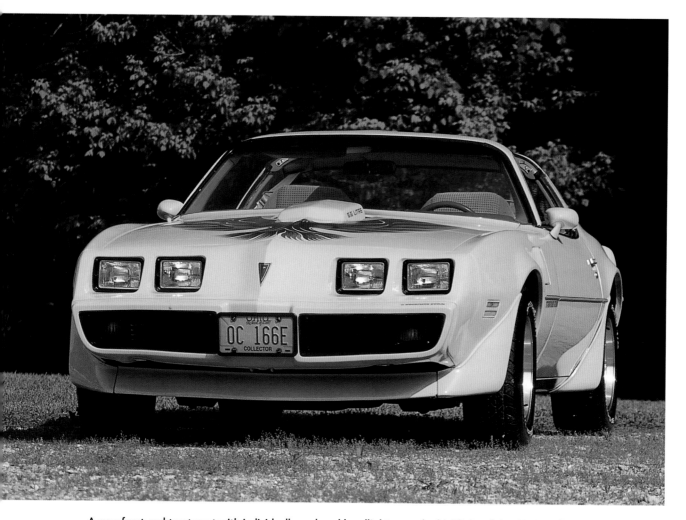

A new front-end treatment with individually enclosed headlights was the highlight of the 1979 Firebird and Trans Am design. The larger, lower black-out openings really gave the front end a new look.

Performance began its comeback with the 1979 model year. Pontiac was still identifying its top 403ci engine with the "6.6 Liter" nomenclature on the shaker top. The net horsepower was rated at 220.

This model year also marked the tenth anniversary of the Trans Am—even though it was actually the eleventh—with the car's appearance and performance both getting a gold star. New-design front and rear fascias, taillights, and air deflectors gave the top model a new look. The standard engine was the Oldsmobile-built 403ci engine. There was even a new bird resting on the hood! The year also marked the permanent return of the SE model, which had a T-top as standard equipment.

To celebrate the anniversary, the company introduced a special model in an edition of 7,500. This was a real looker with silver leather highlighting the interior, unique hood detailing, and special wheels. Put it all together and it was the best-ever production total year for the Trans Am.

This commemorative Trans Am model had both positive performance and appearance going for it. The power under the hood was pretty impressive, at least for the time period, with a 403ci, 220-horsepower power plant.

1980

Appearance packages came on strong again in 1980, with a Yellow 'Bird option on the Esprit and a total of three packages for the Trans Am and Formula. From the standpoint of appearance, the line was relatively unchanged from the 1979 model, although there was a domed hood design that contained a turbo-charged engine with a trio of small lights that progressively illuminated as the turbo boost increased.

A big shuffle took place under the hood for the 1980 model year, with a single V-6 and four V-8s offered. A new 3.8-liter (231ci) Buick-designed V-6 offered a punchy performance and fewer stops at the gas station but kicked out only 115 horses. The five-liter 305ci power plant was available at three horsepower levels. Big blocks? Forget about it.

A trio of 4.9-liter engines displayed horsepower levels of 140, 155, and 210. The latter version, the code T Turbo, really kicked up the power.

The turbo power plant used a unique spark-control system that helped it run close to peak combustion pressures. The turbo boost was maintained at about 9 psi as the turbocharger came up to higher speed so that overboost wouldn't occur. The compression ratio was listed at 7.5:1, with 345 lbs-ft of torque.

1981

The 1981 models were considered the last of this design generation of the Firebird line, and, as such, the model has always remained pretty much unchanged.

Excitement was generated, however, by the release of the movie *Smokey and the Bandit II*, starring Burt Reynolds. This served as the motivation for the creation of the so-called Bandit model, a special edition Trans Am, of which 200 were built. The model featured an upgraded engine, was coal black in color, and was artfully highlighted with gold pinstriping.

There were three versions of the 4.9-liter power plant available in 1980. The Code W standard version was capable of 140 horsepower. Then came the Code Y version, which provided an additional 15 ponies. But the killer is shown here: The turbo version, which kicked out an impressive 210 horsepower.

The front-end treatment for the 1981 Firebird and Trans Am was basically unchanged from the previous year. The lower, pouty snoot protruded far outward, with the four headlights being individually enclosed. This would be the final year for this front-end treatment.

For 1981, the new engine system words were "computer engine control." The stated goal of the system was to provide better fuel economy and lower exhaust emissions, yet still maintain the same level of performance. Doesn't sound like an easy job!

This year also saw the introduction of a new code S 4.3-liter, 265ci V-8. The 5-liter, 305ci four-barrel carbureted engine was available in several versions. Otherwise, few changes were made in the engine lineup for the 1981 model year.

Chapter Five

1982-1992

There was certainly no doubt that with the 1982 model a new era had begun. Everything was different. A new sleekness emerged, one that the Firebird line had never seen before. The era featured three basic models: the basic Firebird, the luxury S/E, and the top-level Trans Am. It was definitely an era of change.

1982

Pontiac advertised the introduction of the l982 Firebird line as the bringing forth of a completely new look and the slickest, most aerodynamic body ever. This first model of the era was accepted by over 116,000 buyers.

The full-race look of this 1983 Trans Am is menacing, to say the least. Note the black lower panel that
completely encircles the car. Also, there are those eyelid headlight slots that go along with the model's overall

The advertising of a completely new look for the 1982 model was certainly justified. The side view of this Firebird provides a look at the new body lines. It was an entirely new look. It should be noted that this particular 1982 Firebird is carrying aftermarket wheels.

The look for the complete Firebird line took on a lower, sleeker style with a completely new front-end design that featured hideaway headlights. Fourteen-inch wheels were standard.

Under the hood, a new four-cylinder, 2.5-liter power plant with fuel injection was the first level of power. Nicknamed Iron Duke, this engine was a killer power plant in racing circuits during the last two decades of the twentieth century and into the twenty-first. A punchy 5-liter V-8, carrying a dual-throttle-body fresh-air system, was also available with the Trans Am.

1983 and 1984

The new look was carried forward for both the 1983 and 1984 models. Even though the

The LG4 5-liter V-8 surprisingly was the largest displacement engine offered for the 1984 model year. In the Trans Am, the power plant was capable of 150 horsepower and perked at a compression ratio of 8.5:1.

This 1984 Trans Am shows a special edition paint scheme. The coal-black model is detailed to perfection with gold, including solid gold body ground effects with parallel pinstriping just above it. Gold detailing is also in place along the upper fender crease lines.

changes were very minor for 1984, the total Firebird production would show a monumental boost to 128,304, of which 55,374 were Trans Ams. Also during this period, the performance image was returning to the Pontiac sports-car line—long overdue, in the opinions of many.

Two special models appeared for this year. The first was the Fifteenth Anniversary Trans Am, which was noted in white and blue graphics. This edition carried many special appointments. Model identification was carried vertically across the doors and on the left headlight door. There was also a so-called Recaro Special Edition,

The rear end of this 1985 Trans Am shows its taut look. The taillights run the complete width, directly under the rear-deck mounted wing. The lower-body effect package is set off with red pinstriping and is quite visible from this view.

in addition to an aero-package option, which closely resembled the Daytona Pace Car models.

With the 1983 model you could experience a kick in the pants when the pedal was crushed to the floor. The quartet of engines that made this possible included a 2.5-liter four-banger; a 5-liter, eight-cylinder with both fuel-injected and carbureted versions; and a pair of impressive 2.8- liter V-6s.

And surprise! That familiar HO designation of earlier days was back in place with the hotter of those V-6s. HO power was just l35 horses, but the

power plant came with custom performance pistons, larger valves, and an 8.9:l compression ratio. Although it sounds far short of the power of the earlier days, recall that there were only 173 cubic inches generating this power compared to the earlier big blocks.

Performance was a missing factor in the 1984 model year, with the 2.5-liter four-cylinder rated at 92 horsepower. A 2.8-liter two-barrel power plant was also available. In addition, there was an HO version of the 2.8 engine, would you believe, mounting only a two-barrel carburetor! But it did get into three figures on the horsepower line with a 125 rating. It carried an 8.9:1 compression ratio. There were a pair of 5-liter mills plus a top L69 150-horsepower version available only with the Trans Am.

1985

The 1985 model year revealed a facelift for both the S/E and Trans Am. The S/E acquired new front- and rear-end treatments, which resulted in a European-style image. The Trans Am, though, benefited most in the change department. Its sleekness became highlighted, with the flashy lower ground-effects package taking the model to the flat-out look of a racecar.

The Trans Am picked up more performance looks with a new lower-aero treatment and fog lights, which were integrated into the front fascia. Available options included 15-inch tires on all models and 16-inch wheels available with the WS6 handling package.

The 1985 Firebird showed a number of upgrades in performance, handling, and appearance. The long-standing model trio—the Formula, the S/E, and the Trans Am—was again in place this model year. Production, though, took a dramatic nosedive, with a total run of 95,880—44,025 of those Trans Ams.

A 2.8-liter Chevy V-6 put some punch back under the hood, pushing out 135 horsepower. Three versions of the 5.0-liter engine provided impressive performance, with 155, 190, and 205 horses, respectively. You could just hear the performance enthusiasts feeling that this added performance was a step in the right direction.

The top two versions of this engine used the more powerful Tuned Port Injection (TPI), and suddenly performance was back online.

Performance improvement was the goal of the 1985 Trans Am. With power plants that featured Tuned-Port Injection and Rally-Tuned Suspension, the model's horsepower reached 205.

1986

A new rear-deck spoiler and a revised hood bird highlighted the upgrades for the Trans Am in 1986. There was also a minor change to the front end for all models, with the return to the twin-grille look. In line with the new safety requirements, a third brake light now rested on top of the hatch.

For the 1986 model year, things were very similar under the hood, with the single 2.8-liter fuel-injected four-cylinder Chevy under the hood. There was practically no change with the three 5.0-liter engines of the previous model year. The 1986 Trans Am even received a new 140-miles-per-hour speedometer.

1987

It was pretty much status quo for the 1987 Firebird models, with the new GTA being the top model designation for the top Trans Am version. The highlights of this model were diamond-spoke, gold-centered wheels and articulated seats.

One would have thought that increased performance in the 1987 models would have attracted more buyers into the showrooms, but it just didn't work out that way. Pontiac made the guess that more punch to the pavement was the answer to lagging sales, and the division would keep trying through the 1991 model year to prove its guess right.

The top-gun Trans Am GTA of 1987 featured a 350ci, 5.7-liter mill, again built by Chevy, which provided a potent 210 horsepower. It had been a long time since such numbers were heard. The competition was the Ford Mustang, which carried a potent 5.0-liter engine. Several different axle ratios were

The front-end treatment for the 1986 Firebird line was slightly changed but retained the same overall look. There was also a new body-stripe treatment. Note the lower gray panel and red striping of this Firebird.

55

The 1986 Trans Am had a molded look to its grille. The parking lights were carried in the lower outer-corner locations, with the Trans Am name printed just above the left parking light. Also note the pair of louvers on the forward portion of the hood.

The GTA was the top dog for Trans Am in 1987, and its classy design is evident from this view. Notice that the taillights are now separate. And those gold honeycomb wheels are dynamite! Note the location of the third stoplight, on the center support of the rear wing.

The "Formula 350" lettering that stretched across both doors identified the top sporty model of the 1988 Firebird line. The model was also accentuated by the complete lower-body black-out treatment. The model was also set off with aluminum wheels and a rear spoiler.

available with the new power plant, which created a potent performance combination.

1988

Pontiac called the 1988 model year "a refinement of the strengths established in 1987." The factory descriptions were the "Fun to Drive Firebird," the "Street Performer Formula" (which returned after a several-year absence), the "Muscular, High-Styled Trans Am," and "The Ultimate GTA."

The GTA was a model in itself for 1988, elevating it above the rest of the Firebird line. It featured a multitude of options, including tuned springs, gas-fueled shocks and struts, and four-wheel disc brakes.

Upgraded to 235 horsepower, the 1988 5.7-liter TPI mill continued to be refined and was the

Power was back with the top engine for 1988. This 5.7-liter (350ci) power plant provided 210 net horsepower. Numerous power train options were available to tailor the power to the buyer's driving style. The engine didn't have the horsepower figures of the good ol' days, but with modern technology, the performance was almost equal to the earlier models.

ultimate potent street performer with 3.27 and 2.77 rear-end gearing available. This power plant was available with two Trans Am models and the Formula. With the GTA Trans Am, the power plant was advertised with an additional five horsepower.

Three 5.0-liter engines demonstrated impressive power options at 170 horsepower, 190 with an automatic, and 215 with the five-speed manual transmission. Choices were everywhere with two other 5.0-liter TPIs available that produced 205 and 230 horsepower, respectively. The 170-horse version of the 5.0-liter also came standard with the basic Formula. The standard Firebird power plant came in the form of a 3.1-liter multiport fuel-injected V-6. It was status quo for Firebird/Trans Am power with the 5.7-liter TPI engine again getting the same 235 horsepower.

1989

The 1989 model year was the two-decade celebration for the Trans Am, even though it was actually the twenty-first model. Regardless, the anniversary model that evolved was out of sight.

A number of changes separated the Trans Ams from previous models, including larger four-wheel disc brakes, aluminum calipers, and huge front and rear stabilizer bars. Coloring

Horsepower was plentiful in 1989 with the 3.8-liter turbocharged power plant. This engine could really put the power to the ground with 14-second quarter-mile performance and quick 0-to-60-mile-per-hour runs.

The 1989 Trans Am GTA was a model with knockout looks. The front end featured the popular aerodynamic curved look with peekaboo headlights and a macho pair of louver sets located on the forward portion of the hood.

was a priority for this machine, with a selection of exterior finishes accented by enameled identification. Trans Ams were also available in three monotone treatments or, if you preferred a more expressive approach, three lower accent colors with contrasting wheel designs were also available.

The 1989 Formula wasn't far behind, as it had a hunky look all its own. The company described it as having "the bulging biceps of a casino bouncer." Available were a power dome hood, aero-wing rear spoiler, and special graphics. The choice between the GTA and Formula would have been a very tough one.

Previous page: Things changed for the Firebird and Trans Am in 1991. The completely new design set the industry on its ear. The classy looking Formula 350 shown demonstrates that new style.

Right: Power was back in fashion, along with the new body design, for the 1991 model. The 5.7-liter TPI turbo power plant was worth 240 net horsepower that could really push this machine down the road!

New horsepower came onto the scene in 1989 with the introduction of the Twentieth Anniversary Turbo Trans Am. The ponies came from a 3.8-liter turbocharged factory-rated 250 horsepower V-6. It was definitely a screamer and demonstrated late-1960s performance with 14-second quarter-mile jaunts along with 0–60 times of five seconds. The model also paced the 1989 Indianapolis 500, a task that it could easily accomplish. It was pronounced in several magazine tests as the quickest model of the year. That was saying something, especially since the Corvette fell into the same testing category.

1990

There wasn't much change in the Firebird lineup for 1990, just minor deviations from the previous year. The Trans Am looked as if it had fallen from favor with the buying public, with only 2,496 built. It's hard to believe that such a great-looking machine could attract so little interest.

The GTA was still the big model for 1990. The long-standing body design had been modernized about as far as it could go, as this was the final year of the body shape that had basically been in place since the early 1980s. To many, though, that design—with its peeking headlights, aggressive front-grille vents, and lower air dam— really set off its image.

In the first model year of the 1990s, the 5.0-liter TPI engine became standard for the Trans Am, and when equipped with an automatic, it was capable of 200 horsepower. With a four-speed in place, the horsepower figure was quoted at 220.

1991

Things turned around in 1991, when Trans Am production doubled and Firebird production increased 13,000 units to 33,832. The increase, though, was not difficult to understand with all the upgrades that were introduced. It was, in fact, a completely new design that took the body to a new level. The biggest change came in the front end, where it was difficult at first look to ascertain that this was indeed a Firebird.

The distinctive GTA aero package for 1991 carried fog lights, brake-cooling ducts in the front fascia, distinctive new side-aero treatment, functional hood louvers, and air extractors. Also standard on the top gun were the WS6 sport suspension and a limited-slip rear end. The Formula was

For 1992 the body style stayed pretty much status quo. The classic sculpturing can certainly be seen down the side of this particular Trans Am.

quite recognizable by its distinctive power bulge hood and specific Formula graphics.

The hot new items for 1991 included convertible options on all models; a new sport appearance package; a new spoiler for the Formula, Trans Am, and GTA; and a new aero treatment for the Trans Am and GTA. New 16-inch charcoal diamond spoke wheels also came with the Trans Am.

For the 1991 model, there were few changes under the hood. The factory didn't explain how each of the standard engines got a five horsepower increase in performance. The 5.0-liter mills were increased to 205 horsepower for the automatic application, while the manual 5.0-liter was now rated at an impressive 230 horses. The 5.7-liter's 240 horsepower really got your attention.

1992

In 1992, it was time to celebrate the twenty-fifth anniversary of the Firebird. The model had stood the test of time and was still standing tall, although it must be admitted that it was still probably in the shadow of the Camaro.

Improvements to the 1992 model weren't visible to the naked eye, but they were extensive under the paint and included the use of more bold welds and increased use of noise-softening adhesives. Externally, there were new body graphics, but with the design changing radically the year before, it was deemed unnecessary to make modifications to this model. In fact, there were no announced performance changes for the 1992 model year. Attention was given to lighter structural components, which, in effect, would accomplish increased performance.

Chapter Six

1993-2002

This final era has seen the rise of a more sophisticated look for the Firebird line. The lower front fascia was uniquely rounded, with the hood curving down to meet it. The peek-aboo headlights were still in place on the front of the hood, but the parking lights now resided in the fascia. Did Pontiac save the best for last? Many think so.

1993

The design situation certainly didn't stand still in 1993, when more than 90 percent of the parts and pieces were new. The model was definitely influenced by the Banshee concept car, which is discussed in chapter 7.

The sweeping lines of the 1993 Firebird and Trans Am received raves from sports car buyers. The side body featured considerable sculpting, which contained an appreciable angle change at the mid-door location. The flashy rear wing was

The front end experienced a huge change, with the grille sweeping into a tight, rounded front with the parking lights located close together in the air dam. The inner edge of the higher-mounted headlights roughly aligned with them. "Swoopy" is the best way to describe that classy hood.

Changes included such elements as a new front bumper system and the reduction of stress concentrations in the body. A heavier use of plastics allowed Pontiac to "twist and flow the body surfaces together in ways never done before." Aerodynamics were greatly improved with pillar under glass, a design in which the windshield wrapped all the way to the side glass, which hid the windshield pillar and enhanced the clean aero look.

Horsepower took a monumental leap up to 275 horses from the 5.7-liter V-8, which was a 35-horse increase over the L98 V-8 it replaced. The Firebird Coupe was powered by the 3.4-liter V-6, which delivered 20 more horsepower and 20 more lbs-ft of torque than the 3.1-liter V-6 used in the former design.

1994

The square-ish look of the 1993 Firebird rear end was replaced by a completely new design in

A serious makeover took place for the 1993 Firebird line. The front end took on a curved, pointed look, with the running lights assuming a round configuration along with being mounted low and close together. Also, the parking lights curved on the outside of the front end. *Pontiac*

66

Note the long, sweeping hood of this 1994 Trans Am. There was certainly a far different look between the Firebird and Camaro lines, which had started off using common sheet metal. The model also sported improvements in suspension and steering.

1994. The rear was now curved, with the tail-lights brought around to the rear quarters. Without doubt, the lines flowed like the wind. Not surprisingly, Pontiac tried to keep the new look for 1994 under cover until the model's official debut. There were photos of the prototype being tested, though, and some slipped out to the public, so the surprise was lost.

The 1994 Trans Am also had a new look, with an aggressive front fascia, integral fog lamps, and rocker panel extensions. All the models also featured polymer composite body panels.

The Firebird line through the years has seen a number of anniversary models, and for 1994, it was time to celebrate the quarter-century mark of the Firebird marquee. It evolved as the

The 5.7-liter LT1 mill assumed its out-of-sight 275 horsepower rating in 1993, and that figure was retained for the 1994 model year. In addition, there was impressive torque, with 325 lbs-ft of rotation performance.

The excellence of the Trans Am design continued for the 1994 version. Many fans consider it one of the best ever. Like in the good ol' days, the company tried to keep the design under wraps and bring it to the public with lots of pomp and circumstance. *Pontiac*

The LT1 engine for the 1994 model year was capable of 275 horsepower. But that kind of performance wasn't for every buyer, as many chose the 3.1-liter SGI V6 power plant shown here. *Pontiac*

Twenty-Fifth Anniversary Trans Am, which carried a blue center stripe and five-spoke rims with center caps. The Trans Am badging was carried on the lower forward doors. There was also a GT Trans Am model, below the GTA, that still was top drawer in appearance.

The 1994 Trans Am retained the 275-horse V-8 and six-speed manual transmission.

1995

In 1995, the Firebird, Formula, and Trans Am all had convertible versions, the first full year of convertible Firebird production since the 1992 model year. The model year did not include a GT model, though.

New features for the big-three 1995 Firebird line featured an optional 16-inch, five-spoke argent aluminum wheel available on certain models. Also, there was traction control, a power antenna, leather interior colors, remote compact disc changer, and a four-spoke steering wheel. Overall external styling, however, remained pretty much the same, a style that has retained its popularity in the following years.

Changes abounded with the 1995 models, including such elements as five-spoke aluminum wheels, traction control, leather interior colors, and a remote compact disc changer. This 1995 Formula shows its lines in great style, including the new look of the grille.

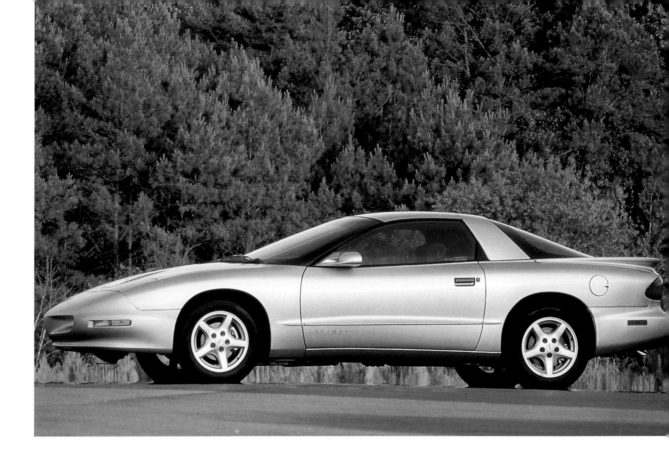

There were very few changes for the 1996 Firebird line, but why would you want to change the magnificence of the Firebird coupe shown here? The WS6 suspension package included 17-inch tires for this model year. Notice the absence of chrome on the sides of this Firebird, which achieved the desired detailing with metal sculpturing. *Pontiac*

The WS6 performance package is shown on this 1996 LT1 engine system. Without the WS6, the engine was capable of 285 horsepower, but with the WS6 the numbers popped to an impressive 305 horsepower.

A new design was introduced for the 1998 Firebird models. One look at the front view of this 1998 Trans Am quickly reveals the differences. The biggest change is manifested in the twin ram-air tunnels that stretch the length of the hood and bring back the good ol' look of the late 1960s and early 1970s.

1996

More refinements for the 1996 line included the five-spoke aluminum wheel being standard on all models. It was also possible to get 17-inch wheels and tires with the WS6 Performance Package. Again, external curves remained basically unchanged.

Changes took place in 1996 when a 3800 Series 11 V-6 was introduced. The 231ci mill was capable of 200 horsepower at 5,200 rpm and 225 lbs-ft of torque at 4,000 rpm. A five-speed manual and four-speed electronic automatic were available with the power plant.

The LS1 5.7-liter V-8 was refined and was capable of an additional 10 horsepower, bringing its rating to 285! It seemed that this potent engine could keep being upgraded with no immediate end in sight.

1997

There were no major body changes instituted in the 1997 model year, but there were refinements, such as a new Monsoon stereo option with a booming 500 watts and the WS6's 17-inch wheels coming in polished aluminum.

A ram-air option was available on the 1997 Trans Am convertible. Pontiac also listed the horsepower rating of the LT-1 with the ram-air system at 305 horsepower. It was rated at 285, as in the previous year, without the ram air.

1998

Big changes were the order for 1998, as all of the major elements of the model were modified. The front end saw a complete redesign, with a more aggressive hood with new front fascias, fenders, and pop-up headlights.

The two fascias featured center twin ports below the hood, with both having newly styled standard round fog lights. A new light bank across the rear included honeycomb tail lamps and round reverse lights. Also, Trans Am and Formula models were equipped with new oval-shaped aluminum exhaust tips. The company noted that the new hood design provided smoother contours and improved the under-hood airflow. The new fender design was common to all Firebird models.

Other upgrades included a new headlight design, honeycomb taillamps with round back-up lamps, leather-wrapped power seats, and air extractors on the front fenders.

The year 1998 also saw the introduction of the new LS1 V-8 engine, which was capable of 305 horsepower at 5,200 rpm, and 335 lbs-ft of torque at 4,000 rpm. It was 20 horsepower and ten lbs-ft of torque greater than the 1997 version. The engine incorporated powder metal

This 1998 LS1 is shown carrying the WS6 ram-air system. This potent combination was capable of producing 335 horsepower at only 4,400 rpm, 20 more ponies than the standard LS1 system. Maximum torque with the WS6 installed was 345 lbs-ft.

rods, an undercut and rolled crankshaft, a high-energy ignition system, and a dye-cast structural oil pan. This engine was standard on the Trans Am, Trans Am convertible, and Firebird Formula Coupe.

1999

The third decade of the Trans Am began in 1999, and the company again saw fit to celebrate a birthday. There were a number of cosmetic additions to the Thirtieth Anniversary model, which makes it highly collectible. The 305

horsepower figure remained in place for the 1999 model year.

2000

For the 2000 models, there was a new hidden headlight design, neatly integrated fog lamps, and fender-mounted air extractors. There were also twin tunnels that cascaded the length of the hood with large openings, harking back to the early days of the model.

The LS1 for 2000 continued on the upward power spiral with 305 horsepower. The increase

Wow! Is this a production machine, or some out-of-sight concept model? It's the former, and it was an available color scheme for the 1999 Trans Am, again going back to the 1969 ram-air Trans Am's look. The macho hood scoops are the distinct trademark of this design.

The 1999 LS1, which had now picked up the Gen III LS1 official designation, continued its evolution, with the top horsepower now quoted at 320. The potent power plant completely fills the engine bay.

came from the addition of a new camshaft and intake manifold. Add on the WS6 Ram-Air system and the ponies vaulted up to 320 at 5,200 rpm. The torque from the ram-air version was impressive at 345 lbs-ft.

The 3800 V-6 engine was also available, an engine that delivered 200 horsepower and 225 lbs-ft of torque. It could be coupled with either a five-speed manual or four-speed automatic transmission.

This 2000 Trans Am looks like the Batmobile going a hundred miles per hour. This coal black version carries the "Ram Air" lettering on each of the functional air-intake ducts. The scoops are a love-hate situation with Firebird enthusiasts.

This rear view of the 2000 Trans Am shows the slight kick-up of the back end with the Firebird symbol rendered in red between the taillights. The design is capped off with the pair of twin-piped dual exhausts, which are fitted into cutouts in the lower bumper.

In addition, this engine featured a sequential-port fuel-injection system.

For the 2000 model, Pontiac did a survey to determine the buyer demographics for the Firebird. It was determined that the median age was 35, mostly male, with a $40,000+ annual income, and some college education. It appeared that the Division was right on the button with its design for that phase of the buying public.

2001

The final-generation look continued for the 2001 model year, and it takes a real Firebird expert to discern the differences between the 1998 through 2001 models.

Just minor changes on the 2001 'Bird, including improved re-valved shock absorbers, which enhanced ride isolation and reduced shake on all models. The Trans Am continued to be offered in

It looked as if this same basic 2001 front-end design would be carried to the expected demise of the Firebird line following the 2002 model year. One thing is for sure: There was certainly plenty of front-end illumination capability with its three different pairs of light systems.

The 5.7-liter power plant just kept getting better and better through the years. This factory photo shows an x-ray photo of the power plant's installation in a 2001 Trans Am. *Pontiac*

The 2001 Gen III LS1 picked up a new camshaft and intake manifold, and this power plant is standard on both the Trans Am and Formula. With its 310 horsepower at 5,200 rpm, the performance could be increased with the ram-air package, which boosted the horsepower figure by 10.

This magnificent model is the 2002 Trans Am Collector Edition. Notice the black emblems and flowing side and hood detailing. The black top and window treatments seem to cascade together. *Pontiac*

convertible editions. Standard equipment included removable roof panels, leather seat surfaces, and an up-level rear spoiler for the coupe.

The Firebird line showed a refined design, which featured a "smoothing" in the front end. The dominant hood scoops of the previous model were eliminated, replaced by a less-aggressive, sleeker appearance. The lower front design, though, remained relatively unchanged with the closely spaced parking lights.

In 2001, five more horses came online with the LS1, that brought its rating up to 310 horsepower, with ram air gunning up to 325. Torque was measured at 350 lbs-ft. The LS1 could be mated with a six-speed manual transmission, which could be equipped with an optional Hurst shifter. The V-6 engine power remained at the 2000 values.

2002

It's official: 2002 is the Firebird finale, but this is certainly not from lack of style and performance. This final thirty-fifth edition could very easily be the best of lot.

The LS1 keeps punching out additional ponies, with the 2002 version getting 15 more, giving it a horsepower rating of 325 with ram air. What more do you have to say?

Minor refinement is the name of the game in 2002, with a smoothing of the front end. The hidden headlight design continues, as do the neatly integrated fog lamps and fender-mounted air extractors. The 2002 Trans Am is offered with standard equipment roof panels with sunshades, leather seating, and an up-level rear spoiler for the coupe.

Chapter Seven

The Race
Connection

If there is a General Motors Division that is associated with motor sports, it's Pontiac. This is true for many reasons. First, there is the Trans Am, which has been a perennial pace car in both NASCAR and Indy car. Then, there was the Formula Firehawk performance model and other aftermarket models that seemed like they would be more at home on a racetrack than the street.

But getting down to actual racing, the Firebird in its early days was a participant in the Sports Car Club of America (SCCA) Trans-Am series. And although the model never won the series, it was very competitive against brutal competition. During the 1970s and

A field of IROC Firebirds thunder through turn four at Talladega in an April 1996 race. The cars were made as equal as

1980s, the Firebird showed strong in short-track stock car competition. It also competed in such pony car circuits as the American Speed Association (ASA) and the ARTGO series. In the International Race of Champions (IROC) series, it was Firebirds—equally prepared race Firebirds—that carried the world's greatest drivers to compete against each other. The Firebird body style has also been a dominant factor in national drag racing, particularly in The National Hot Rod Association (NHRA) Funny Car competition. And finally, the Trans Am has had some amazing world record performances running in a straight line.

Indianapolis 500 and NASCAR Pace Cars

There were a limited number of the tenth-anniversary models garbed as Daytona 500 Pace Cars, which are obviously rare and more desirable for collectors. But the kingpin for the 1980 year

This factory photo shows the 1989 Indy 500 Pace Car posed on the track on the Victory Lane platform before the big race. Being named the Indy 500 Pace Car is a huge publicity benefit, and this pace car model made the most of it. *Pontiac*

was the Indy 500 Pace Car X87 model, a specially detailed Trans Am with Brickyard graphics on both sides. There was also a small Indy 500 logo below the Trans Am lettering on the lower front quarters. The pace cars carried the 4.9-liter turbo power plant and were a popular seller, with approximately 5,600 built.

The pacer was white with a charcoal accent color extending from the hood through the upper door, the front of the sail panel, and the forward half of the roof. Red and charcoal striping was the final accent. Silver-tinted removable hatch-roof panels and aluminum white air-flow wheels were standard equipment. Along with the turbo 4.9-liter power plant, the pacers toted the three-speed automatic transmission and a 3.08 rear axle.

Does the Trans Am ever get tired of being a pace car? Well, apparently not! In 1989 the Indy honor was again bestowed upon it. But national exposure or not, the Trans Am production fell to approximately one-fourth of its 1988 level, with only 5,358 sold.

The Pace Car Edition, of which there were only about 1,500 built, generated an impressive 245 horses from a 3.8-liter turbocharged Buick V-6 engine hooked to a four-speed automatic.

The pace car replicas were almost identical to the real pacers externally, missing only the strobe lights of the race day models. From a performance standpoint, the model didn't have to be modified for its pacing duties. The performance was advertised as having a 13.8-second capability in the quarter and a 150-mile-per-hour top speed.

Another race commemorative model came forth with the 25th Anniversary Daytona 500 Pace Car. The Recaro Trans Am was a highly detailed gold and black beauty that carried a $3,610 additional cost when the crossfire-injected 5.0-liter engine was ordered.

Race-Performance Street Trans Am Vehicles

Probably more than any other 1990s muscle-sports car, the Firebird and Trans Am were used

Trans Ams have long been the selection of NASCAR for pacing duties at its Winston Cup races. Here, a 1993 Trans Am shows off its NASCAR pace car garb, ready for the 1993 Daytona 500. Trans Am and pace car have gone together for a long time. *Pontiac*

by aftermarket performance companies to make the models as great as they could be. Engine and appearance tweaks made them considerably more expensive—and highly collectible. The SLP Firehawk and MMS Supercar are two prime examples of this type of upgrading.

The SLP Firehawk

Starting with the 1992 model year, Pontiac, with the assistance of SLP Engineering, introduced its amazing Firehawk, a niche-performance street Firebird. For the years it was produced, it could actually be purchased with pure-race equipment, including such features as no rear seat, a super-light aluminum hood, racing-style Recaro seats, huge front disc brakes, and a Simpson five-point front harness. It cost an extra five figures for all this good stuff, but if you wanted your Firehawk full-race, you just had to do it!

Eldora Speedway in Ohio uses a beautifully detailed 1993 Trans Am for its pacing duties. *Darrell Willrath*

Under the hood, it was just like the good old big-block days, with that same type of performance being coaxed from a small-block 5.7-liter Chevy that pumped out 350 horsepower. The mill was pure race, with aluminum pistons, a forged crank, four-bolt mains, and stainless steel headers. Not only did the engine have the horsepower, it also provided huge torque at 390 lbs-ft. For this kind of performance with all the goodies, you could tie close to $50,000 into this hauler. You were effectively getting Corvette performance from a Firebird-type machine, something that concerned the GM brass.

For the 1993 model, the Firehawk was defeathered a bit down to 300 horsepower and given a considerable reduction in price. Even still, the Firehawk was capable of 13.5 second quarter-mile runs at 103 miles per hour. Zero to 60 came in less than five seconds with the Firestone 17-inch SZ tires. Much of the modification work was accomplished by SLP Engineering, and it would also have a part in the 1994 model, which it also modified.

For 1994, SLP added a classy free-breathing exhaust, which added 15 horses, and an optional suspension system ($1,500 extra) dropped the model another inch. The system also increased the grip and greatly reduced the body roll.

SLP kept molding the Firehawks through the mid-1990s, with 500 built in 1994 and an additional 671 the following year. That latter model reportedly had 13-second quarter-mile performance and 150-mile-per-hour top speeds. In 1995, SLP was also responsible for an upgraded Trans Am, called the Comp TA.

During the 1996 and 1997 model years, SLP was involved in the design of the factory ram-air systems of the two years.

This specially prepared 5.7-liter, capable of pumping out 350 horsepower, was the power for the 1992 Formula Firehawk. It carried a four-bolt main, forged crank, aluminum pistons, and stainless steel headers. It's better than the good ol' days, with its 350 horsepower and 390 lbs-ft of pavement-scorching torque. Zero-to-60 performance was an awe-inspiring 4.9 seconds. Throughout the years the Firehawk has been a performer of the top order, one of the hottest production machines ever produced in this country.

The modifications have continued through the years, with more Firehawks manufactured for the 2001 and 2002 model years. The latter model used a 345-horsepower version of the LS1 engine.

MMS Supercar

Morgan Motorsports (MMS) produced a 2001 Trans Am-based street machine, which carries a so-called full-race 421 SD power plant that is capable of an inspiring 625 horsepower. From an appearance standpoint, the MMS vehicle has given the front of the vehicle a brand new, totally smooth look.

The suspension is completely altered to race standards, but the model retained the stock T-56 transmission and 3.42 geared rear end. Performance is inspiring, with four-second 0 to 60 timing and 11.4-second/127-mile-per-hour capabilities in the quarter-mile.

continued on page 90

85

Firebird/Trans Am Concept Cars

Perhaps more than any other General Motors model, the Firebird line has probably had more concept models developed using its design influence. Following are some of the highlights.

XP-836 Concept Firebird

In fact, this was an initial concept car that Pontiac had hoped would serve as the basis for the first Firebird. Conceived in the early 1960s as a Mustang fighter, the XP-836 Project initial design was mandated as a four-seater, something that Pontiac engineers didn't like.

XP-833 Concept Firebird

Thus, a second design came along, coined the XP-833, which made all other designs look like blocks of wood. It was a sleek open-wheel beauty, far ahead of its time in a design sense, and as it worked out, it was just too far ahead. When it was presented to the top brass, it was quickly discarded. There were rumblings at the time that if the model had been produced, it could have threatened the GM's flagship, the Corvette.

Firebird Type K Sportwagon Concept

Yep, the firebird was supposed to be a sporty car, but you would never have realized that from the Firebird Type K Sportwagon concept car that emerged in 1978. The Type K was a mini-station wagon with the roofline extended at the same height to the rear of the vehicle.

The future looks of the Firebird are apparent in this photo of the 1988 Banshee concept car. *Pontiac*

Projected sticker prices of some $20,000—which was huge in that day—doomed the design from ever being produced.

Banshee Concept Car

In 1988, Pontiac introduced a sleek concept machine called the Banshee. It was stated at the time that the model "was designed as a futuristic performance coupe." Construction was based on a steel tubular frame fitted with a fiberglass body.

The Banshee rear used integrated lower airfoils with deck-mounted split wings to govern air flow. All exterior glass was flush-mounted and the body was absent of all door handles and mirrors. Power came from a four-liter DOHC engine rated at 230 horsepower at 5,600 rpm.

Pontiac Sunfire Concept Car

In 1990, a Firebird-influenced concept car called the Sunfire was introduced. It was defined as a racy, performance sport coupe on the outside with an open interior spaciousness that seated four adults comfortably.

The major refinements of the vehicle were accomplished on the inside with a floating console, under which the front seats could adjust forward or back. The console contained the radio, CD, heater, and air-conditioning controls.

With a 109-inch wheelbase, the design featured carbon fiber panels, two-part doors, 20- and 21-inch wheels, and composite high-level headlights. Power was provided by a 2.0-liter, 16-valve DOHC turbo-charged 190-horsepower engine.

Protosport4 Concept Car

This 1991 design used the Firebird as the starting point—a V-8 powered, high-performance,

The 1990 design of the Sunfire Concept Car showed tendencies that would evolve in production models later in the decade. Note the rakish angle of the windshield, which really gives this model a great aerodynamic coefficient figure. *Pontiac*

rear-wheel-drive machine. The philosophy was to acquire as sophisticated and new-looking a car as was possible.

Desiring a racing image, the design featured doors derived from Le Mans-type race cars of the 1960s and 1970. The driver's pod enabled the

The 1991 Protosport4 Concept Car again shows its Firebird design influence in the front-end design. *Pontiac*

projection of instrument panel images to much larger than normal size. Projected were big, simple analog gauges. The body was completely fabricated of carbon fiber panels, with the power coming from a 4.0-liter double-overhead-cam fuel-injected V-8 with an electric-shift automatic transmission.

Sunfire Speedster

In 1994, Pontiac introduced another Sunfire machine called the Sunfire Speedster. Also showing its Firebird roots, this concept machine was a follow-on to the earlier Sunfire concept vehicle. One major difference, though, was the new 225 horsepower, 2400-cc twin-cam, 16-valve supercharged ram-air-inducted power plant. Also featured was an electronically controlled four-speed automatic transmission.

Mongoose Concept Car

In 1996, Pontiac showed another concept car, this one based on a 1996 WS6 Firebird. The model carried the stock LS1 engine augmented with an SLP performance exhaust system, with other power train components consisting of a Hurst shifter, aluminum drive shaft, and finned aluminum rear end cover. The suspension was further augmented with a larger front sway bar, Koni double adjustable shocks, and much stiffer springs. Because it was built specifically for race applications, the model omitted all unnecessary equipment, such as air conditioning, speakers, rear seat, and even the radio antenna.

Pontiac Rageous Concept Car

The final concept with a Firebird connection was the Rageous concept machine first shown in 1997. This was a radical, brutish machine that "was bulging with muscle and bold Pontiac excitement," according to the company. It's not unlike the look of the front of the 2001 Firebird and Trans Am models.

Although the Rageous had a sport-look to it, there was also a significant hauling capability— very un-sporty—as the rear cargo volume of the machine could accommodate 4x8 sheets of plywood.

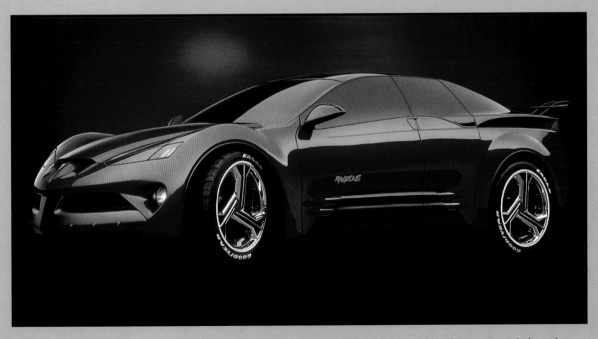

The Rageous Concept Car might more logically be named "Outrageous," with its startling design. Nevertheless, that front end found its way into the 2000/2001 Firebird production design. *Pontiac*

Continued from page 85

Racing Series Involving Firebird Models

Not only has Pontiac been on the track in the aforementioned pace car capacity, but it has also competed in a pair of national racing series, the SCCA Trans-Am and IROC series.

SCCA Trans-Am Series

Unlike Chevy with the Z28 Camaro model, Ford with the BOSS 302, and Chrysler with the T/A Challenger, Pontiac did not introduce a special model to publicize its Trans-Am racing participation.

But the company did initiate a low-level effort with a 1967 Firebird racer powered by a 230ci six-cylinder topped with three single-barrel Weber Carbs. It was a curious choice of power plants in a land of powerful V-8s. The model was never produced in a street version.

However, the power plant for one 1968 Trans-Am Firebird used a Chevy Z-28 engine that had been built in Canada. It was a perfectly legal situation for Trans-Am qualification since the engine was manufactured out of the country. The use of this engine was required at the time since Pontiac had no small-block V-8 available to it.

There was also a short-term deal in the late 1960s when Pontiac decided to de-stroke its 400ci power plant down to 303 cubes. The power plant carried high-compression ram-air heads and two four-barrel carbs. The mill reportedly made more than 475 horses, well in excess of the Camaro competition. But the required numbers were not produced, so Chevy 302 Z28 engines were substituted.

The early Firebird Trans Am racer weighed about 3,350 pounds and carried a front suspension that sported independent upper and lower control arms, front coil springs, a rear live axle, and leaf springs.

The Firebird team played in the point finishes of two drivers in the 1968 season. Sharing a

Mustang and Firebird, Jerry Titus finished third in the Trans-Am points. But it was Craig Fisher who showed Firebird's colors with a fourth-place finish in the points, done mostly in a 'Bird, but with a few races in a Camaro. The Firebird finishes included two seconds, one third, and two fourths.

In 1969, Titus ran the whole season in a Firebird and finished third in the points with one win, three thirds, two fourths, and a fifth. Milt Minter brought home a tenth-place points finish with two fifths and a pair of tenths. In 1972, Minter was the pride of Pontiac, finishing runner-up in the points.

The Firebirds that ran from the 1970 to 1972 time period used a Chevy 305ci engine with a single four-barrel and 450-plus horsepower. The models carried four-speed transmissions, forged steel spindles, and four-wheel disc brakes.

The year 1983 was a great one for Pontiac and Elliott Forbes-Robinson, who ended up fourth in the points, and Frank Leary, who followed in fifth. Both drove Trans Ams. In 1985, the final time Pontiac would play in the Trans-Am points, Bob Lobenberg ended up fifth in the points, while Jim Miller was seventh.

There were significant Firebird accomplishments in the manufacturers points. In 1982, Pontiac won the Manufacturers Championship after placing second the prior year. It took third-place finishes in 1969, 1972, 1978, 1984, and 1985.

IROC Racing Series

In 1996, Pontiac became involved with the International Race of Champions (IROC) series, a racing series with a different approach. Where all other racing series had separate teams working to make their cars superior to the competition, the IROC series has all its cars prepared by the same team working to make each as equal as humanly possible.

The reason for that goal is to provide a fleet of cars that can serve as a measure of driving skills for a group of drivers from many different areas of the racing world. The IROC series races in four events annually on NASCAR tracks.

The Firebird body style provides the factory identification for Pontiac, but under that close-to-stock body shell lies a potent race car. Using small-block Chevy power capable of 500 horsepower at 6,800 rpm, speeds of 190 miles per hour have been achieved at the super speedways. This pack of Firebirds—driven by skilled hands—provides some of the highest numbers of contestants in worldwide racing.

Short Oval-Track Racing

For many years, the Firebird and Trans Am have been vigorous performers in short-track racing in both the United States and in Canada. In fact, during the 1970s and into the 1980s, many circuits were almost completely Camaro and Firebird oriented. When a number of body styles were introduced in the mid-1980s, the Pontiac models remained solid contenders.

Most of these short-track machines were fiberglass replicas of the Firebird/Trans Am body shapes, and with the exception of fender

This Pontiac factory photo shows the detailing on the IROC Firebird race car. Externally, the car used stock lines, but needless to say, there was no way that you could ever buy one of the cars off the showroom floor! *Pontiac*

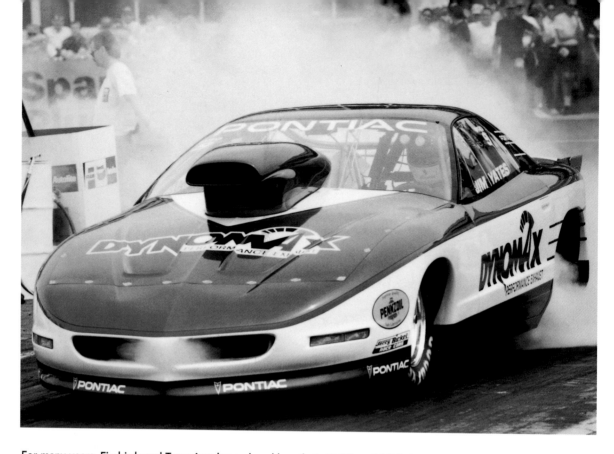

For many years, Firebirds and Trans Ams have played heavily in NHRA and IHRA drag racing. Longtime Super Stock driver Jim Yates drove this 1993 Firebird Formula-bodied drag machine during the 1993 season. *Pontiac*

flares and wider wheel cutouts for the wide racing tires, the racers were very close to stock contours. The power plants used in these machines were either a 350ci V-8 or a smaller V-6. The Firebird and Trans Am models competed in such national series as ARTGO, ASA, ACT, All-Pro, and others.

The big name with Firebirds during the 1970s was former NASCAR driver Dick Trickle. Running with the ARTGO circuit, Dick turned to Firebirds in 1977 and ran them until 1980. Over that time he brought the Pontiac logo to the checkered flag 21 times. There was also a string of seven consecutive wins in 1979. Trickle also won the ARTGO championship in both 1977 and 1979.

NHRA/IHRA Drag Racing

The Firebird lineage has also played in the national drag racing scene with participation in both the national NHRA and IHRA circuits.

Since the early 1990s, the NHRA participation has included Rickie Smith, Jerry Eckman, and Jim Yates in Pro Stock competition. More recently, Warren Johnson has been Pontiac's main man in NHRA Pro Stock, with titles in Firebirds coming in 1998 and 1999, along with eight national speed records, 27 national event wins, and six national elapsed-time records.

In NHRA Funny Car competition, a number of heavy hitters have driven the Firebird brand, names such as John Force, Don Prudomme, Al Hofmann, Cruz Pedregon, Randy and Shelly

Firebirds were a heavy participant in ASA racing during the 1970s and 1980s. Here, veteran racer Butch Miller pushes his Firebird to the front in a 1985 ASA race. *David Tucker*

Probably the fastest Firebird ever, this 1999 model was modified by Kugel and LeFever for a straight-line run of just over 300 miles per hour at the Bonneville Salt Flats in Utah. *Pontiac*

Anderson, Cory McClanathan, Bruce Allen, Jim and Jamie Yates, Tom Martino, and Mark Pawuk, among others.

In the early 2000s, the Firebird Funny Car body is still a favorite choice.

Local Drag Racing

Even at the local level, at the hundreds of local drag strips across the country, more often than not you will see new and old Firebirds and Trans Ams doing their thing. They are two of the most popular contenders at this level of Saturday night hometown racing.

Land Speed Racing

During the mid-1980s, Don Stringfellow set a new world land-speed record for stock passenger cars of 260.21 miles per hour at Utah's Bonneville Salt Flats in a Trans Am prepared by Gale Banks Engineering.

In an amazing 1991 speed effort, Dave Macdonald pushed his 1991 Trans Am to the A Gas Coupe speed mark at the Bonneville Salt Flats, reaching a speed of 268.799 miles per hour. Had he not encountered mechanical problems, there could well have been a 300-mile-per-hour run. The Trans Am also shattered the nitrous category record with a 272.203-mile-per-hour clocking.

Macdonald indicated that the Trans Am body style was aerodynamically superior to any other available. "Since I wasn't allowed to change the bodylines, the car ran just the way it came from the showroom and it performed extremely well," he said. In August 1999, Joe Kugel, driving the Kugel & LeFevers twin-turbo Pontiac Firebird, reached an average speed of 300.788 miles per hour, representing the first production-based car to exceed the 300-mile-per-hour milestone.

In 2000, John Rains, driving a highly modified 1989 Trans Am, set a record in the E/PS Class by reaching a speed of 256.789 miles per hour.

Endurance Racing

Pontiac began its association with IMSA's Street Stock Endurance class in 1985. Doug Goad and his father, retired Pontiac Special Engineering Manager Tom Goad, campaigned a specially prepared Trans Am for the Wheel-to-Wheel, Inc. racing team. After one second-place finish out of five raced in 1985, the duo won the 1986 Sebring Six-Hour endurance race, registering the first American professional racing win by a father-son driving team. Over the years, Doug Goad has secured 33 career race wins and logged over 40,000 miles in Firebirds.

Index

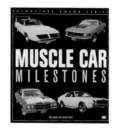
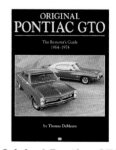